The Eiffel Tower Fascinating Facts For Kids

Leanne Walters

All rights reserved. No part of this publication may be reproduced in any form or by any means, including scanning, photocopying, or otherwise, without prior written permission of the copyright holder. Copyright Leanne Walters © 2020

This book is just one of a series of "Fascinating Facts For Kids" books. For more fascinating facts about people, history, animals, and much more, please visit:

www.fascinatingfactsforkids.com

Contents

The Idea.. 1
Gustave Eiffel...............................4
The Design..................................... 7
Construction.............................. 10
Completion................................. 18
Temporary or Permanent?.......... 21
The Tower Today........................ 24
Assorted Eiffel Tower Facts..........26
Illustration Attributions...............29

The Idea

1. In the late nineteenth century, France was recovering from decades of war and violence that had started in 1789 with the French Revolution. The Revolution saw the overthrow of the monarchy and the establishment of a republic, a system of government where the people get to choose who rules them.

2. The last two decades of the nineteenth century saw France once again at peace and becoming a prosperous and powerful country. It was decided to hold a huge fair in the French capital, Paris, to show off modern France to the rest of the world. The fair – known as the "Exposition Universelle" - would celebrate French technology and engineering. It would be held in 1889, the 100th anniversary of the French Revolution.

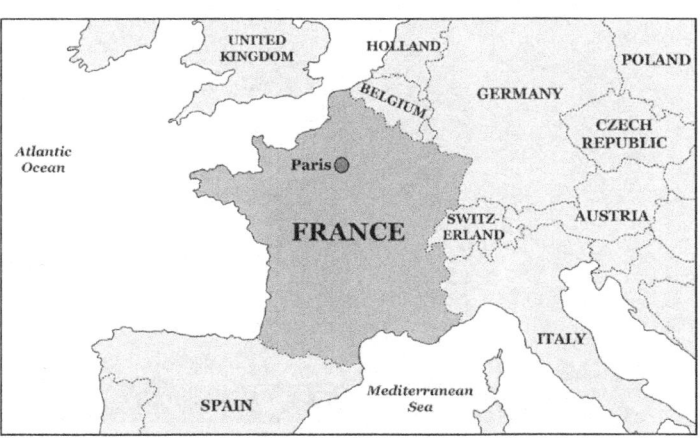

3. The organizers of the Exposition wanted a great symbol to show off French engineering, and it was decided to build a huge tower which would be the tallest structure in the world. The world's tallest structure at the time was America's *Washington Monument*, which stood 555 feet (169 m) high. The new tower in Paris would be nearly twice as high, soaring almost 1,000 feet (305 m) into the air.

The Washington Monument

4. The Exposition organizers decided to hold a competition for French engineers and architects to submit their ideas and designs for the tower. There were more than 100 entries and the winner was fifty-three-year-old Gustave Eiffel, one of France's finest architectural engineers.

Gustave Eiffel

Gustave Eiffel

5.   Alexandre-Gustave Eiffel was born in Dijon, France, on December 15, 1832. He was interested in construction and architecture from an early age, and after leaving school he enrolled in engineering college in Paris.

6.   In Paris at the time, architects were beginning to construct buildings from iron rather than stone, and Eiffel became fascinated by metal and its many possibilities.

7.   After graduating from college in 1855, Eiffel worked on the construction of iron bridges, before starting his own company in 1866. His reputation grew, and soon he was building bridges and other structures in countries across the world.

8.   Between 1882 and 1884, Eiffel and his company built the highest bridge in the world. The *Garabit Viaduct* is a railroad bridge made from iron, and it crosses a valley 400 feet (120 m) above the Truyère River in Central France.

The Garabit Viaduct

9. Eiffel became famous in 1886, when the *Statue of Liberty* was opened in New York Harbor. The statue was a gift from the people of France to the United States to celebrate American independence in 1783. Eiffel was responsible for the huge metal skeleton around which the *Statue of Liberty* was built, and which has supported the statue for more than 130 years.

The Statue of Liberty

The Design

10. Eiffel worked with his top architects and engineers to come up with a ground-breaking, unique design for the tower. The base would be made from four huge, inward-sloping legs. On top of the base, 184 feet (56 m) above the ground, would be a platform from which the rest of the tower would rise, getting narrower as it rose 984 feet (300 m) into the air.

An early drawing of the tower

11. The tower would be made from more than 18,000 pieces of wrought iron – which is both strong and flexible – all held together by 2.5 million rivets. The iron pieces would be made in Eiffel's factory, before being taken to the construction site to be put together.

12. Because the tower would be so high, Eiffel and his team had to design it to withstand the force of the wind. The tower was built to be aerodynamic in shape, so that the wind could flow smoothly past without causing damage. It would be built not as a single, solid structure, but from a network of crisscrossing iron beams. The spaces between the beams would allow the wind to pass through easily.

Crisscrossing iron beams

13. On January 8, 1887, Eiffel signed a contract to build the tower. There were just over two years before the Exposition was due to open, and many people thought it would be impossible for Eiffel to complete such an ambitious project in time. But he had worked everything out in great detail and was confident about the challenge ahead.

Construction

14. Work began on the building of the *Eiffel Tower* on January 28, 1887, with the laying of the foundations. The tower's four legs would rest on massive slabs of concrete set deep underground. These foundations would support the colossal weight of the finished tower.

15. The tower was to be built on land next to the River Seine, but Eiffel soon realized he had a problem. Two of the tower's legs would stand close to the river, but the ground there was wet clay, too soft to support the weight of the legs.

16. Eiffel got his workmen to dig holes deeper into the ground until they reached clay that was drier and more solid. The holes were then filled with concrete to form foundations that would be strong enough to stop the legs from sinking into the ground.

The Eiffel Tower foundations

17. While the foundations were being laid, the thousands of iron pieces that would form the tower were being made at Eiffel's nearby factory. In July, the first pieces arrived at the construction site in horse-drawn carts, and the building of the tower could begin.

18. The tower would be built from the ground up, with the four legs being assembled first. The iron pieces were put into place and connected to each other with rivets - which are special metal bolts that are heated and hammered into shape to securely join two or more pieces of metal.

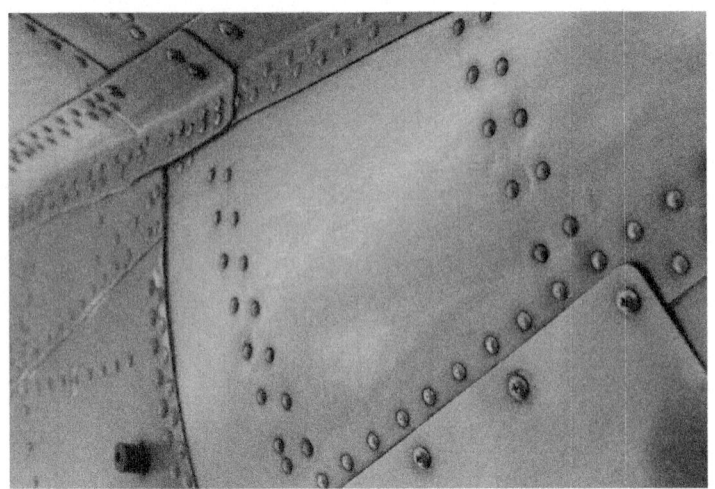

Rivets connecting pieces of metal

19. As the legs grew taller, wooden scaffolding was erected to support the growing weight. It became more and more difficult to lift heavy pieces of metal into place, so special cranes and hoisting machines were used.

The legs being built

20. When the legs were finished they were joined to each other by building a huge, square platform on top of them. This platform - 187 feet (57 m) above the ground – would be the first floor of the tower and be the base from which the rest of the tower would be built.

The finished legs

21. The first floor was completed in April 1888, just a year before the Exposition was due to open. Eiffel knew he was in a race against time, and so he got his men to work for up to twelve hours a day, seven days a week. He even installed a canteen in the tower so that his workers wouldn't waste time going all the way to the ground for their meals.

22. By August 1888, the tower had risen to a height of 377 feet (115 m) where the second floor was added, and by the following March the tower had reached its full height of 984 feet (300 m).

The completed second floor

23. Although there would be stairs all the way to the third floor of the tower – which was the top floor, 906 feet (276 m) above the ground - Eiffel knew that most people would not want to climb such a long way, so he decided to install elevators.

24. Installing the elevators was one of the biggest challenges that Eiffel faced. The elevator industry at the time was fairly new, and Eiffel was unsure if they would work in his tower.

25. A French company was able to install elevators between ground level and the first floor, but the shape of the tower between the first and second floors presented problems which they couldn't solve.

26. Eiffel was not allowed to use foreign materials in the construction of the tower, but no French company wanted to undertake the work on the first and second floor elevators. In the end, an American elevator company had to be brought in to solve the problems, and Eiffel eventually got a reliable elevator system.

One of the tower's elevators

27. Now the construction of the tower was nearly finished, Eiffel had it painted. He chose a reddish-brown color and told his painters to use lighter shades as they got higher in order to make the tower look even taller than it actually was.

Completion

28. By the end of March 1889, the *Eiffel Tower* was finally finished, and Gustav Eiffel and some important guests climbed the 1,710 steps to the top floor of the tower. They stopped frequently on the way, and when they eventually reached the top an hour later, Eiffel hoisted a huge French flag to celebrate his remarkable achievement.

29. Because of problems with the elevators, the tower didn't open to the public until May 15, nine days after the opening of the Exposition. But when it finally did open it became a huge hit with the public. During the six months that the Exposition was open, nearly two million people visited the tower, including a record 23,000 on one day alone.

30. People flocked to the *Eiffel Tower* to take in the spectacular views over Paris and the surrounding countryside. In the days before airplanes, only mountaineers and balloonists had been to high altitudes, so the experience of looking down at the ground from nearly 1,000 feet (305 m) high was a new experience for most people.

The view of Paris from the Eiffel Tower

31. As well as enjoying the views, visitors could also eat at one of the tower's four restaurants and buy souvenirs in the tower's shops. At the top of the tower there was a small post office from which visitors could send postcards and letters as a memento of their visit.

32. After dark, visitors on the top floor of the tower could shine powerful spotlights down on the buildings and monuments of Paris. The whole tower was illuminated by hundreds of gas lamps, and an electric lamp at the very top of the tower sent out red, white, and blue beams of light – the colors of the French flag.

The tower after dark during the "Exposition Universelle"

Temporary or Permanent?

33. The *Eiffel Tower* had been intended to be a temporary structure, and was due to be dismantled in 1909, twenty years after it had been built. But Eiffel wanted his tower to stand permanently, and thought that if he could prove the tower's usefulness to science, then he could prevent it from being torn down.

34. In the late nineteenth century, long distance communication was difficult or slow, with letters taking weeks to arrive in a faraway country. The telegraph and Morse Code could send messages instantly, but thousands of miles of wires and cables needed to be laid across land and under oceans for the messages to travel along.

35. In 1896, an Italian inventor named Guglielmo Marconi found a way to transmit messages through the air using radio waves, which were sent and received by electrical devices called antennas. Eiffel was fascinated by radio waves and knew that the height of his tower made it ideal to send and receive messages from.

Guglielmo Marconi

36. With the help of a French scientist called Eugène Ducretet, Eiffel installed an antenna high up on the third floor of his tower. On November 5, 1898, a radio message was sent from the *Eiffel Tower* to a building three miles (5 km) away.

37. In 1899, Eiffel successfully sent a message across the English Channel to London, England, more than 200 miles (320 km) away. He also persuaded the French Army and Navy to use his tower to send messages to their forces overseas. To Eiffel's delight, the importance of the tower in sending and receiving radio waves persuaded the

Paris authorities to save the *Eiffel Tower* from being dismantled.

The Tower Today

38. Today, the *Eiffel Tower* is one of the world's most popular tourist attractions. Around seven million people visit the tower every year, an average of nearly 20,000 people a day. Since it opened in 1889, more than 250 million people have visited the tower.

The tower today

39. The tower is not quite the same as it was when it first opened. The elevators today are faster and there are more shops. A glass floor has been installed on the first floor, nearly 200 feet (69 m) above the ground. There is even an ice rink for visitors to skate on during the winter months.

40. The hundreds of gas lamps that illuminated the tower in 1889 have been replaced by 20,000 electric light bulbs. Every night, they are switched on for five minutes every hour to provide a spectacular light show which can been seen from all over Paris.

The tower at night

41. The *Eiffel Tower* needs regular maintenance, including completely repainting it every seven years to stop the iron from rusting. It takes twenty-five people between fifteen and eighteen months to complete the job.

42. The color of the *Eiffel Tower* has changed many times over the years. Today it is painted in three shades of brown, with the darkest shade at the bottom and the lightest shade at the top. The use of three different shades makes the tower blend in with the Paris sky.

Assorted Eiffel Tower Facts

43. The Mayor of Blackpool, England, was a visitor to the "Exposition Universelle" in 1889, and was so inspired by the *Eiffel Tower* that he commissioned a similar structure to be built when he got home. The *Blackpool Tower* opened in 1894, although at 518 feet (158 m) tall it is half the size of the *Eiffel Tower*.

The Blackpool Tower

44. The *Eiffel Tower* was the world's tallest structure for forty years. The 1,046-feet-high (319 m) *Chrysler Building* in New York City took the title in 1930, being sixty-two feet (19 m) taller than the *Eiffel Tower*. The *Chrysler Building* held the record for just eleven months, when the 1,250-feet-high (381 m) *Empire State Building* opened in New York.

The Chrysler Building & the Empire State Building in the 1930s

45. Unusually for such a huge building project, no workmen were killed during construction thanks to the safety precautions Eiffel put in place. The only person to die was a worker who fell to his death while showing off to his girlfriend at night when the tower was closed.

46. Eiffel paid for most of the construction of the tower himself, with the French authorities contributing around a quarter of the costs. As Eiffel was risking so much, it was agreed that he could keep any income from visitors to the tower. The tower proved so popular that Eiffel made his money back in less than a year.

47. Before building the *Eiffel Tower*, Gustave Eiffel had been responsible for the construction of more than forty bridges and viaducts, as well as playing a major part in the building of the *Statue of Liberty*. But the *Eiffel Tower* was the pinnacle of his career and made his name famous throughout the world. Gustave Eiffel died on December 27, 1923, at the age of ninety-one.

Illustration Attributions

Gustave Eiffel
USMC Archives from Quantico, USA / CC BY
(https://creativecommons.org/licenses/by/2.0)

The Garabit Viaduct
Graeme Churchard / CC BY
(https://creativecommons.org/licenses/by/2.0)

An early drawing of the tower
Maurice Koechlin, Émile Nouguier / Public domain
{{PD-US}}

The Eiffel Tower foundations
Musée d'Orsay / Public domain
{{PD-US}}

The legs being built
Unknown author / Public domain
{{PD-US}}

The finished legs | The completed second floor | One of the tower's elevators
{{PD-US}}

The tower after dark during the Exposition
Georges Garen / Public domain
{{PD-US}}

Guglielmo Marconi
Pach Brothers / Public domain
{{PD-US}}

Blackpool Tower
Nathanemmison / CC BY-SA
(https://creativecommons.org/licenses/by-sa/4.0)

The Chrysler Building in the 1930s (Fact 44)
Library of Congress / Public domain
{{PD-US}}

Printed by Amazon Italia Logistica S.r.l.
Torrazza Piemonte (TO), Italy

66124830R00020